SCRIPT: Xavier Dorison & Fabien Nury · Drawing & Colour wor

SPOOKS

3. El Santero

9th CINEBOOK
The 9th Art Publisher

MORTON CHAPEL

A complicated man, he might have been content with being English and a connoisseur of Fu Long tea... And yet, the head SPOOK is as skilled in the study of the occult as he is at handling a "Schofield" model Smith & Wesson.

JOEY BISHOP

A sharpshooter and the team's veritable killing machine, he fears only one thing: his feelings for Kathryn Lennox.

BART TRUMBLE

An enforcer so burly and imposing that some people tend to forget Bart also has a brain and a heart. And yet, both are in perfect working order.

KATHRYN LENNOX

The daughter of an immensely wealthy Republican senator, she could have settled for the peaceful life offered to a young woman. Except that Kathryn Lennox, a psychiatrist trained by Freud, isn't the kind to meekly follow the beaten path...

ANGEL SALVAJE

This Catholic Indian, learned in exorcism rituals, is one of the few people to know Morton Chapel well, as he's been a member of the team for years.

RICHARD CLAYTON

Sponsor and commander of the SPOOKS, he takes orders directly from the President of the United States. The only thing as strong as his cynicism is his ability to adapt...

---

15 FEBRUARY 1898. The armoured cruiser *USS Maine* explodes in Havana Bay. In response to this 'aggression', the President of the United States Robert McKinley decides to intervene in Cuba, in order to free the island from the Spanish yoke and bring it democracy.

10 JUNE 1898. Nearly 300,000 American troops, among them Theodore Roosevelt, invade Cuba.

The Treaty of Paris of 10 December 1898 brings the war to a close. Spain renounces its sovereignty over the island. A military government is set up by the Americans. No Cubans were present at the signing of the treaty.

1902. American troops, reinforced by the Cuban Guardia Civil, are still there. While 'democratic' elections are organised on the island, still only one flag flies over Havana…

Original title: W.E.S.T. 3 – El Santero
Original edition: © Dargaud Paris, 2006 by Dorison, Nury & Rossi
www.dargaud.com - All rights reserved
English translation: © 2013 Cinebook Ltd - Translator: Jerome Saincantin

Lettering and text layout: Design Amorandi - Printed in Spain by Just Colour Graphic
This edition first published in Great Britain in 2013 by Cinebook Ltd
56 Beech Avenue - Canterbury, Kent CT4 7TA - www.cinebook.com - A CIP catalogue
record for this book is available from the British Library - ISBN 978-1-84918-170-9

9th CINEBOOK
The 9th Art Publisher

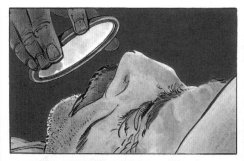

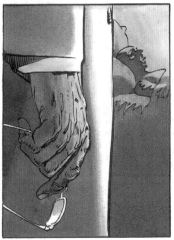

CUBA,
7 JANUARY 1902

LORD, WE BEG YOU TO ACCEPT YOUR HUMBLE SERVANT EDWARD NASH AT YOUR SIDE, FOR HE WAS A GOOD AND GENEROUS MAN.

AS PRESIDENT OF THE UNITED FRUIT, HE WORKED HIS WHOLE LIFE FOR THE FREEDOM AND PROSPERITY OF THE CUBAN PEOPLE. AND EVEN THOUGH HE WAS AN AMERICAN CITIZEN, HE REQUESTED TO BE BURIED HERE, IN THIS COUNTRY HE CHERISHED.

I AM THE RESURRECTION AND THE LIFE: HE THAT BELIEVETH IN ME, THOUGH HE WERE DEAD, YET SHALL HE LIVE.

GENERAL WOOD! GENERAL! IS EDWARD NASH'S DEATH THE WORK OF A SANTERO AS MOST CUBANS BELIEVE?

IS IT BECAUSE OF THAT DEATH THAT YOU HAVE JUST OUTLAWED THE SANTERIA RELIGION?

EDWARD NASH DIED OF YELLOW FEVER. IT IS A TERRIBLE DISEASE, AND THE UNITED STATES ARMY IS FUNDING THE GREATER PART OF THE RESEARCH AGAINST IT...

...AND NONE OF THIS HAS ANYTHING TO DO WITH SANTERIA OR ANY OTHER SUPERSTITION!

GENERAL! WAS EDWARD NASH MURDERED BY THE INFAMOUS ISLERO YOUR SOLDIERS HAVE BEEN HUNTING FOR MONTHS?

COME NOW, MY FRIENDS...

SPEAKING FOR ALL SHAREHOLDERS OF THE UNITED FRUIT, I CAN ANNOUNCE THAT THE DEATH OF OUR FRIEND EDWARD NASH WILL IN NO WAY CHANGE THE POLICIES OF OUR COMPANY...

DIRECTOR, IS IT TRUE THAT THE ARMY HAS PLACED YOU UNDER INCREASED PROTECTION?

...WHICH WILL CONTINUE TO WORK FOR THE ECONOMIC AND SOCIAL DEVELOPMENT OF OUR BEAUTIFUL ISLAND OF CUBA.

MR JOHNSON, SINCE YOU ARE GOING TO REPLACE EDWARD NASH, AREN'T YOU AFRAID FOR YOUR LIFE?

ER... NO COMMENT...

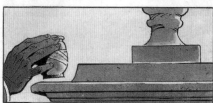

I WANT THIS GRAVE GUARDED DAY AND NIGHT.

YES, COLONEL... BUT WHY?

DAY AND NIGHT! DO YOU HEAR? I HOLD YOU PERSONALLY RESPONSIBLE FOR THIS TASK, CORPORAL DELSOL!

AT YOUR COMMAND, COLONEL WEYLER.

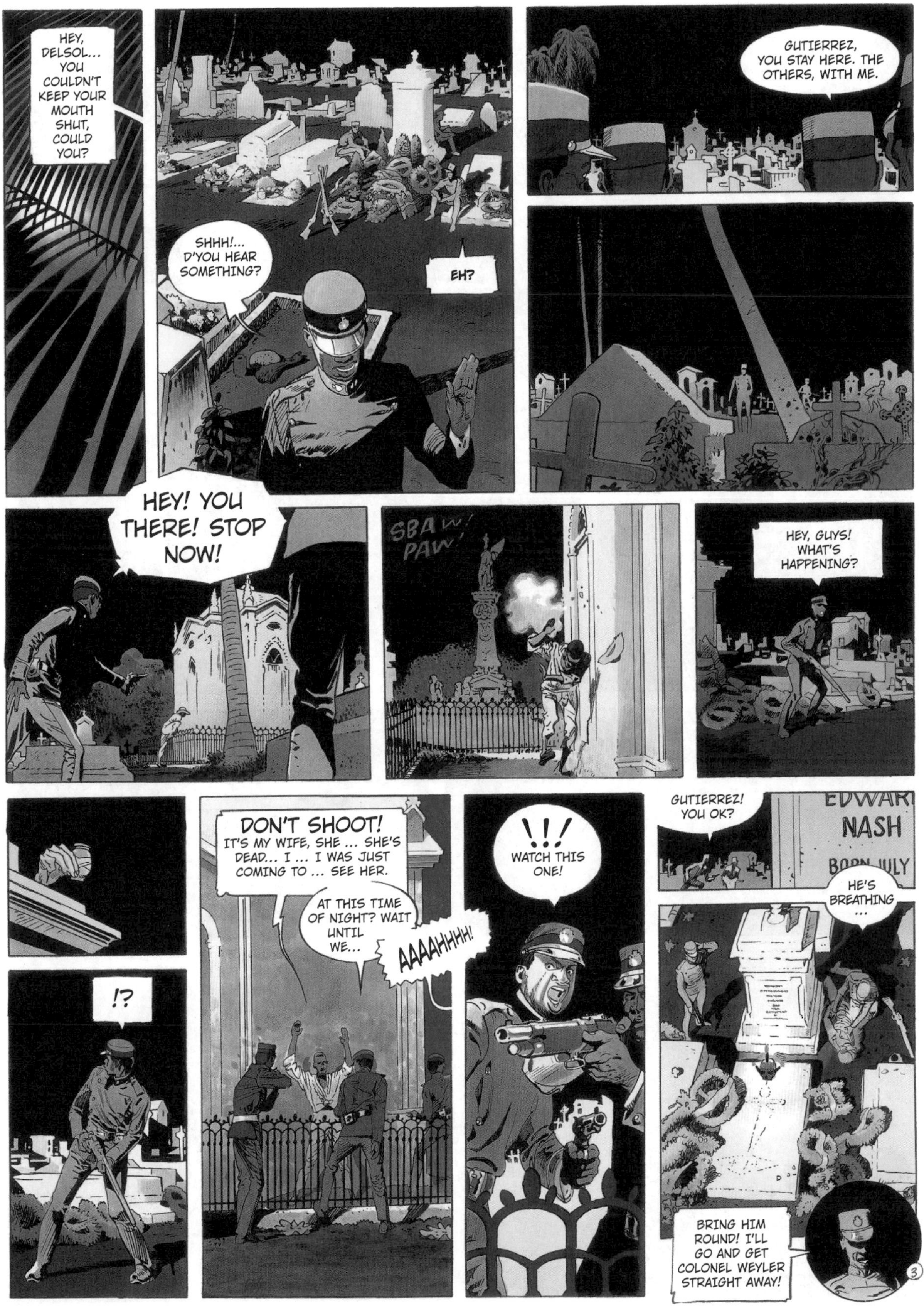
HEY, DELSOL... YOU COULDN'T KEEP YOUR MOUTH SHUT, COULD YOU?
SHHH!... D'YOU HEAR SOMETHING?
EH?
GUTIERREZ, YOU STAY HERE. THE OTHERS, WITH ME.
HEY! YOU THERE! STOP NOW!
SBAW! PAW!
HEY, GUYS! WHAT'S HAPPENING?
!?
DON'T SHOOT! IT'S MY WIFE, SHE ... SHE'S DEAD... I ... I WAS JUST COMING TO ... SEE HER.
AT THIS TIME OF NIGHT? WAIT UNTIL WE...
AAAAHHHH!
!!!
WATCH THIS ONE!
GUTIERREZ! YOU OK?
EDWAR
NASH
BORN JULY
HE'S BREATHING ...
BRING HIM ROUND! I'LL GO AND GET COLONEL WEYLER STRAIGHT AWAY!
3

...AND WE TOOK A PRISONER, COLONEL. MUST BE ONE OF THOSE REVOLUTIONARIES!

DIG UP THE COFFIN!

I GAVE YOU AN ORDER, SOLDIER! DIG UP THAT COFFIN AND OPEN IT!

RIGHT AWAY, COLONEL, SIR!

AAAARGH IT STINKS!

HOLY MARY MOTHER OF GOD! ...

ISLERO.

4

...THE TELLER AMENDMENT GAVE US A CLEAR MANDATE: WE WERE TO FREE CUBA FROM THE SPANISH YOKE ... AND FOUR YEARS LATER, WE'RE STILL THERE!!! WE WERE LIBERATORS; WE'VE BECOME OCCUPIERS!

OF COURSE, I CAN ALREADY HEAR MY REPUBLICAN COLLEAGUES BOASTING OF THE 'DEMOCRATIC' ELECTIONS THAT ARE FINALLY GOING TO TAKE PLACE... BUT THEN WHY IS THIS ASSEMBLY AWASH WITH FOUL RUMOURS? RUMOURS OF PLAIN AND SIMPLE ANNEXATION?

HAVE WE FORGOTTEN ALL THE PRINCIPLES WE PURPORT TO DEFEND?... ARE WE GOING TO FLOUT OUR CONSTITUTION TO SERVE THE INTERESTS OF A HANDFUL OF WHEELER-DEALERS?

ARE WE GOING TO RENEGE ON OUR COMMITMENTS AND MAKE A NATION OF LIARS OF AMERICA?

SENATOR SPAAKHAAS IS IN FINE FORM TODAY.

HE CAN YAP AS MUCH AS HE WANTS, HE'S STILL IN THE MINORITY!

ALL THOSE WHO WORK AND MAKE THE DECISIONS IN CUBA WANT ANNEXATION! IT'S ONLY AN AGITATOR OR TWO WHO ARE GETTING THE NEGROES AND MULATTOS WORKED UP WITH THEIR VOODOO NONSENSE...

SANTERIA.

...IF YOU WISH.

PRESIDENT ROOSEVELT BELIEVES THAT ANNEXATION ISN'T A GOOD SOLUTION...

ROOSEVELT HAD BETTER THINK HARD IF HE WANTS TO KEEP OUR SUPPORT! CUBA MADE HIM, BUT CUBA COULD ALSO DESTROY HIM... AFTER ALL...

...HE WAS NEVER ELECTED!

I DID NOT ORGANISE PRESIDENTIAL ELECTIONS IN CUBA FOR SOME EXTREMISTS TO WIN THEM. DO YOU UNDERSTAND ME, CLAYTON?

PERFECTLY, MR PRESIDENT. IT'S ALSO THE OPINION OF SENATOR GRAY...

THE OPINION OF THE UNITED FRUIT, YOU MEAN...

ALL RIGHT, LISTEN CAREFULLY: WE HAVE TO GET RID OF THAT WITCH DOCTOR, THAT **ISLERO**... SIX MONTHS AGO NO ONE KNEW HIM, AND NOW HE'S ALL THE CUBANS TALK ABOUT!... UNLESS SOMEONE STOPS HIM, WE COULD LOSE THE ELECTIONS!

THE SPOOKS ARE ON THE CASE, MR PRESIDENT. IF **ISLERO** IS REAL, THEY WILL FIND HIM ... AND WILL MAKE SURE THE CUBANS FORGET HIS VERY NAME!

⑤

7

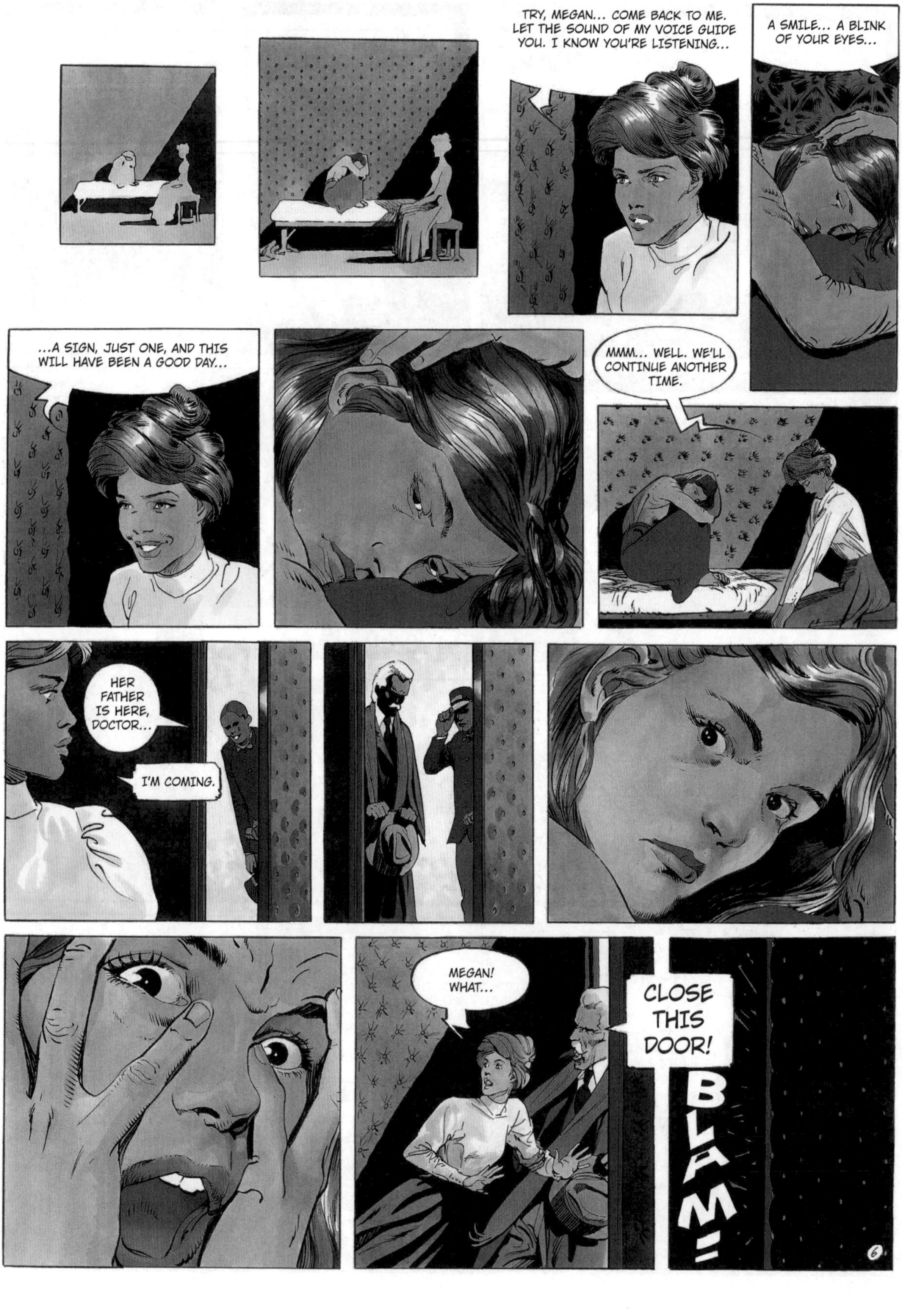
TRY, MEGAN... COME BACK TO ME. LET THE SOUND OF MY VOICE GUIDE YOU. I KNOW YOU'RE LISTENING...
A SMILE... A BLINK OF YOUR EYES...
...A SIGN, JUST ONE, AND THIS WILL HAVE BEEN A GOOD DAY...
MMM... WELL. WE'LL CONTINUE ANOTHER TIME.
HER FATHER IS HERE, DOCTOR...
I'M COMING.
MEGAN! WHAT...
CLOSE THIS DOOR!
BLAM!
6

YOU... YOU CAUSED HER TO REACT! AS SOON AS SHE SAW YOU! IT'S...

IT'S YOU I CAME TO SEE, NOT HER!

ROOSEVELT AGREED: YOU'RE NOW PART OF THE TEAM.

WHAT ABOUT MEGAN? DON'T YOU WANT TO HELP HER? UNTIL YOU TELL ME EXACTLY WHAT HAPPENED, THERE'S NOTHING I CAN DO FOR HER!

WE'RE LEAVING FOR CUBA. MEET US AT GRAND CENTRAL TONIGHT AT TEN O'CLOCK. WE'LL TAKE THE TRAIN TO MIAMI, THEN A SHIP TO HAVANA. PACK LIGHT. COURIER WILL PROVIDE WHAT WE NEED.

AND YOUR DAUGHTER?!?

MEGAN CANNOT BE CURED.

9

WANT TO SHARE?

EXCUSE ME?

YOUR ... CORDIAL, IS IT RUM?

IT'S MEDICATION.

NEVER MIND. FORGIVE THIS RATHER CAVALIER INTRODUCTION ...

....JOEY BISHOP, CULINARY CRITIC FOR THE *BALTIMORE GOURMET*. I'M GOING TO WRITE AN ARTICLE ON CUBAN CUISINE. HOW WOULD YOU LIKE TO KEEP ME COMPANY AT A GOOD TABLE?

YOU'D RUIN MY APPETITE!

NICE TO MEET YOU, LADIES. BART TRUMBLE, IMPORTER OF COMBINE HARVESTERS – THE FUTURE OF AGRICULTURE!

HOW INTERESTING... IS THIS YOUR FIRST TRIP TO CUBA?

THE FIRST OF MANY, I HOPE...

I'M HERE TO BRING THE SUGAR-CANE TRADE INTO THE 20TH CENTURY...

...NOTHING LESS.

YOUR ANALYSIS, DOCTOR?

SIMPLE. NASH'S BODY WAS NEVER IN THE COFFIN.

I AGREE COMPLETELY.

THAT'S A FIRST... DON'T YOU BELIEVE IN VOODOO?

I NEVER SAID THAT. I AGREE WITH YOU THAT NASH'S BODY WAS NEVER ACTUALLY IN THE GRAVE. AND FOR YOUR INFORMATION, CUBAN VOODOO IS CALLED **SANTERIA**.

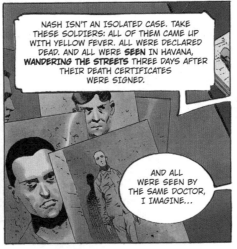

NASH ISN'T AN ISOLATED CASE. TAKE THESE SOLDIERS: ALL OF THEM CAME UP WITH YELLOW FEVER. ALL WERE DECLARED DEAD. AND ALL WERE **SEEN** IN HAVANA, **WANDERING THE STREETS** THREE DAYS AFTER THEIR DEATH CERTIFICATES WERE SIGNED.

AND ALL WERE SEEN BY THE SAME DOCTOR, I IMAGINE...

INDEED. DR CARLOS FINLAY, THE US ARMY'S MEDICAL OFFICER IN HAVANA.

PROMISE ME ONE THING... IF I HAPPEN TO BE SICK, DON'T TAKE ME TO SEE THAT GUY!

NOW, MISS LENNOX...

MMM?

I WANT YOU TO WEAR THIS ON YOUR WRIST.

ARE YOU JOKING?

I NEVER JOKE.

THIS IS PARANOID FETISHISM!

THIS IS PROTECTION... A CUBAN FRIEND GAVE ME THIS BRACELET DURING MY LAST TRIP THERE; IT SAVED MY LIFE!

YOU KNOW, THAT'S PRECISELY WHAT I **HATE** ABOUT ALL THOSE CHARLATANRIES: THE WAY YOU INTIMIDATE PEOPLE TO PUSH THEM INTO BELIEVING ALL YOUR **NONSENSE!**

BART HAS HIS. BISHOP HAS HIS. DO YOU THINK I INTIMIDATED BISHOP?

BISHOP? REALLY? THAT'S NOT HIS STYLE...

BISHOP PROVED REASONABLE FOR ONCE... HE TOLD ME: 'I DON'T BELIEVE IN GHOSTS ... BUT I'VE SEEN THEM.'

WEARING THAT BRACELET DOESN'T MAKE A SUPERSTITIOUS MORON OUT OF HIM. OR YOU... BUT IF I HAPPENED TO BE RIGHT AND YOU REFUSED IT ... WE COULD ALL COME TO REGRET IT.

OH? WELL, I WAS EXPECTING...

...A MAN OF COURSE.

IF YOU'D LIKE TO FOLLOW ME... THE GENERAL ORDERED THAT YOU BE SPARED HAVING TO GO THROUGH CUSTOMS.

THANKS SOLDIER, BUT WHY DON'T YOU TAKE CARE OF DR LENNOX'S 15 BAGS INSTEAD...?

MR CHAPEL? I'M CAPTAIN MORROW, GENERAL WOOD'S AIDE-DE-CAMP. DR LENNOX ISN'T WITH YOU?

I AM DR LENNOX.

EVERYTHING'S IN ORDER, MR BISHOP. WELCOME TO HAVANA.

GOOD... TELL ME, IS THERE ONE OF YOUR SUPERIORS HERE I COULD HAVE A WORD WITH?

I'D LIKE TO REPORT A SUSPICIOUS INDIVIDUAL.

HEY, EASY! THESE MACHINES ARE WORTH A FORTUNE!

IF YOU'D CARE TO WAIT HERE... THE GENERAL WILL SEE YOU IN A MOMENT.

...THE MOMENT'S PASSED!

BUT!... YOU CAN'T DO THAT!

FLASH

⑩

12

AND NOW IT'S RUINED!

! WHO GAVE YOU THE RIGHT?...

PRESIDENT THEODORE ROOSEVELT.

OF COURSE. IT'S A STRATEGY OF APPEASEMENT! THE CUBAN PEOPLE NEED TO KNOW THAT THEY ARE NOT ALONE IN THESE TROUBLED TIMES.

MMM, GENERAL... WE'D NEED AT LEAST ONE CONVINCING PHOTOGRAPH...

I DOUBT THE GENERAL WILL HAVE THE TIME NOW, MISTER...

...TOMÁS ESTRADA PALMA, LIBERAL CANDIDATE TO THE CUBAN PRESIDENCY.

FORGIVE MY CURIOSITY, MR PALMA, BUT ... ARE YOU SURE SUCH A CAMPAIGN WILL BE EFFECTIVE WITH THE CUBANS?...

TOMÁS... IF YOU WOULDN'T MIND...

BUT OF COURSE! WE WERE THINKING OF TAKING A FEW PICTURES IN THE RECEPTION LOUNGE ... WEREN'T WE, ALFONSO?

DON'T ASK ME, I'M JUST THE TECHNICIAN!

WELL, MAKE YOURSELVES COMFORTABLE, PLEASE.

SO IT'S YOU THE WHITE HOUSE SENT TO GET IN MY WAY! AS IF I COULDN'T SORT THIS BUSINESS OUT BY MYSELF!

HAVE YOU RECOVERED EDWARD NASH'S BODY?

NO... THAT WOULD HAVE BEEN TOO MUCH TO ASK FOR. BUT WE ARRESTED A NATIONALIST REBEL IN THE CEMETERY THAT SAME NIGHT... A MAN NAMED CIANEGA.

YOU'LL BE ABLE TO QUESTION HIM. HE'S PROBABLY A CLOSE ASSOCIATE OF THAT ISLERO CHARACTER ... ASSUMING HE EXISTS.

...BUT I WANT TO SPEAK WITH NASH'S WIDOW. AS FOR DR LENNOX, SHE'S VERY EAGER TO MEET HER COLLEAGUE DR FINLAY. THAT'S THE MAN WHO TAKES CARE OF THE BEWITCHED SOLDIERS?

SICK! THE SICK SOLDIERS! DR LENNOX WILL BE TAKEN TO THE MILITARY CAMP'S INFIRMARY. WHAT ELSE?

NO NEED. IF YOUR MEN WEREN'T ABLE TO MAKE HIM TALK ABOUT ISLERO, I DON'T SEE HOW WE COULD MANAGE IT...

⑪

13

THAT WILL BE ALL FOR NOW.

MMM... VERY WELL. I HEARD ABOUT YOU, YOU KNOW...

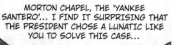

MORTON CHAPEL, THE 'YANKEE SANTERO'... I FIND IT SURPRISING THAT THE PRESIDENT CHOSE A LUNATIC LIKE YOU TO SOLVE THIS CASE...

...ESPECIALLY AS I'VE ALREADY TAKEN ALL NECESSARY MEASURES...

SUCH AS YOUR DECREE BANNING THE PRACTICE OF SANTERIA UNDER PAIN OF IMPRISONMENT?

ABSO-LUTELY!

I THOUGHT THAT FREEDOM OF RELIGION WAS ONE OF THE FOUNDATIONS OF DEMOCRACY.

THAT'S TRUE ... FOR AUTHORISED RELIGIONS.

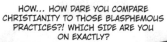

GENERAL, HOW IS YOUR KNOWLEDGE OF CHRISTIAN HISTORY?

I HAVE SOME EDUCATION – AND I AM A PRACTISING CHRISTIAN.

THEN YOU MUST KNOW THAT THE ROMAN EMPIRE, TOO, TRIED TO OUTLAW CHRISTIAN BELIEFS IN ITS TIME... AND WHERE ARE THE ROMANS NOW?

HOW... HOW DARE YOU COMPARE CHRISTIANITY TO THOSE BLASPHEMOUS PRACTICES?! WHICH SIDE ARE YOU ON EXACTLY?

I HAVE A MANDATE FROM THE PRESIDENT OF THE UNITED STATES TO...

¡VIVA ISLERO! ¡VIVA EL SANTERO!

ARREST HIM! ARREST THAT MAN!

SBAM SBAM

PWWWWW

12

14

13

*IRISH REPUBLICAN BROTHERHOOD: AN ORGANISATION DEDICATED TO THE ESTABLISHMENT OF AN INDEPENDENT DEMOCRATIC REPUBLIC IN IRELAND. ITS US COUNTERPART EVENTUALLY BECAME KNOWN AS THE FENIAN BROTHERHOOD.

THE VERY LATEST IN TERMS OF MODERN PRINTING! THIS GEM CHURNS OUT 170 POSTERS AN HOUR. ENOUGH TO COVER EVERY WALL OF HAVANA – OR RESUME PRINTING YOUR NEWSPAPER...

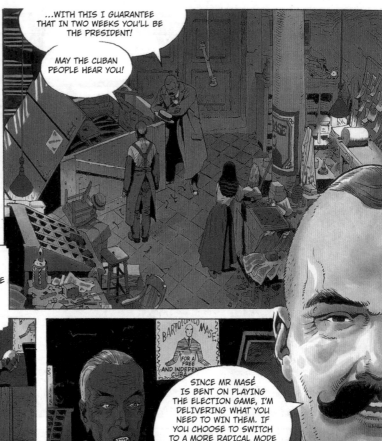

...WITH THIS I GUARANTEE THAT IN TWO WEEKS YOU'LL BE THE PRESIDENT!

MAY THE CUBAN PEOPLE HEAR YOU!

AND YOU DON'T WANT TO BE PAID? I'M HAVING A HARD TIME UNDERSTANDING SUCH GENEROSITY!

NOT GENEROSITY, LIL' LADY; THINKING AHEAD. ONE DAY YOU'LL BE IN POWER, AND ON THAT DAY THE **IRB** WILL STILL BE IN NEED OF FRIENDS IN HIGH PLACES. D'YOU KNOW WHAT I MEAN?

SINCE MR MASÉ IS BENT ON PLAYING THE ELECTION GAME, I'M DELIVERING WHAT YOU NEED TO WIN THEM. IF YOU CHOOSE TO SWITCH TO A MORE RADICAL MODE OF ACTION, I CAN ALSO PROVIDE THE NECESSARY SUPPLIES...

...NOW, IF YOU DON'T LIKE MY EQUIPMENT, I CAN TAKE IT BACK.

I DARE YOU!

WE'RE TAKING IT! AND WHATEVER HAPPENS, WE WILL STICK TO THE ELECTORAL GAME – I'LL LEAVE THE 'RADICAL' MODE TO YOU.

LOVELY. I HOPE YOUR OPPONENTS WILL HAVE THE SAME SCRUPLES. RIGHT, I SUPPOSE YOU'LL BE WANTING PAPER TOO?

?! BY SAINT PATRICK!

THE GUARDIA CIVIL! YOU TRICKED ME!

! I SWEAR WE DIDN'T!... IT'S YOU WHO...

IS THERE ANOTHER EXIT?

THE INNER COURTYARD.

GO! I'LL HOLD THEM BACK!

14

AND YOU?

I HAVE MY PAPERS AND I'M AN AMERICAN CITIZEN. THEY'LL NEVER...

...AAAAAR

HELP! OOOMPF! I'M BEING ATTACKED!

FREEZE OR I'LL SHOOT! YOU'RE UNDER ARREST!

YOU HAVE NO RIGHT! I'M AN AMERICAN!

THE GUARDIA THANK YOU, MR BISHOP.

I ONLY DID MY DUTY, LIEUTENANT.

STEP ONE ... COMPLETED.

16.24
...

...PLEASE NOTE THE TIME OF DEATH. IDENTITY OF THE DECEASED: CORPORAL HERBERT SCHENCK, 5TH INFANTRY REGIMENT, US EXPEDITIONARY CORPS. CAUSE OF DEATH: YELLOW FEVER.

ARE YOU CERTAIN OF THAT, DR CARLOS FINLAY?

!?! I BEG YOUR PARDON, MISS...

DOCTOR. DR KATHRYN LENNOX. GENERAL WOOD SHOULD HAVE INFORMED YOU I WAS COMING. ARE YOU CERTAIN OF YOUR DIAGNOSIS?

SEE FOR YOURSELF, DR LENNOX...

...NO PULSE, NO BREATHING, NO INVOLUNTARY REACTIONS. THIS MAN IS DEAD.

WELL, WE'RE IN AGREEMENT ON THAT POINT... AND THE YELLOW FEVER? WHAT WERE THE SYMPTOMS?

HIGH FEVER FOLLOWED BY PERIODS OF REMISSION; VOMITING LACED WITH BLOOD; YELLOW TINT TO THE SKIN INDICATING THE LIVER WAS DAMAGED. WHAT MORE DO YOU WANT?

AND THESE MARKS?

SIMPLE MOSQUITO BITES.

IS THERE ANYTHING ELSE FOR YOUR SERVICE, DR LENNOX? I HAVE MANY PATIENTS.

YES, BUT ONLY ONE COMMANDER: GENERAL WOOD...

...BE NICE TO HIM: FINISH YOUR ROUNDS THEN COME AND HELP ME IN MY RESEARCH.

WHICH CONCERN...?

YOUR 'SPECIAL CASES'.

16

WE HAD TO ISOLATE THEM FROM THE REST OF THE SICK.

TO PRESERVE TROOP MORALE, I IMAGINE?

MIGHT AS WELL TRY TO GO TO THE MOON. ALL THE SOLDIERS HEARD ABOUT IT AGES AGO. YOU CAN IMAGINE THE EFFECT THAT HAD ON THEM...

PARANOIA AND SUPERSTITION HAVE ALWAYS GONE WELL TOGETHER, DR FINLAY. YOU MUST FEEL RESPONSIBLE ...

WHY IS THAT?

WELL, YOU'RE THE ONE WHO SIGNED THOSE ERRONEOUS DEATH CERTIFICATES...

ERRONEOUS?! BUT I WOULD SIGN THEM AGAIN, EVEN AFTER SEEING THOSE MEN WALK ABOUT HAVANA! THEY WERE JUST AS DEAD AS THE ONE YOU EXAMINED!

COME, DOCTOR, YOU KNOW AS WELL AS I DO THAT...

I KNOW WHAT I SAW. I AM A MAN OF SCIENCE. AND EVEN THOUGH I AM CUBAN, I BELIEVE IN NEITHER ZOMBIES NOR ANY FORM OF REVENANTS!!!

THAT SAID, I MUST ADMIT THAT THESE ONES...

...ARE RATHER CONVINCING.

MRS NASH, PLEASE ACCEPT MY MOST SINCERE CONDOLENCES. THANK YOU FOR GIVING ME A FEW MOMENTS. I KNOW THAT THIS ISN'T THE BEST TIME.

I'M LISTENING, MR CHAPEL.

ACCORDING TO HIS MEDICAL FILE, YOUR HUSBAND HAD ALREADY HAD YELLOW FEVER?

YES, A YEAR AGO. HE'D BEEN GIVEN QUININE, AYER'S PILLS AND MAGNESIUM CITRATE. EVERYTHING HAD RETURNED TO NORMAL, BUT THIS TIME ... THE DRUGS DIDN'T HELP.

MADAM, I REALISE MY QUESTION MAY SEEM INAPPROPRIATE ... BUT HAD YOUR HUSBAND RECEIVED ANY THREATS?

MY HUSBAND WAS ADORED BY ALL HIS EMPLOYEES! HE WAS GENEROUS, RESPECTED AND POPULAR!

17

I DON'T DOUBT IT, BUT ... PERHAPS YOU'VE NOTICED SOME SORT OF SIGN? TRACES OF ASH ON THE DOORSTEP? A MARK PAINTED ON YOUR FLOOR OR WALLS? THE DISAPPEARANCE OF PERSONAL OBJECTS – HAIR BRUSHES, JEWELLERY, BROOCHES?... OR MAYBE AN ITEM THAT WOULD HAVE BEEN DELIBERATELY LEFT IN YOUR HOME?

JOSE, SHOW MR CHAPEL WHAT WE RECEIVED.

BUT SEÑORA ...

YES! YES! I KNOW! YOU DON'T WANT TO TOUCH IT!

WE GIVE THEM WORK, WE BUILD THEM ROADS, SCHOOLS ... AND WHAT DO THOSE INGRATES GIVE US IN RETURN?

THIS!

THOSE BASTARDS AT THE UNITED FRUIT DON'T WANT US TO TALK ABOUT IT! BUT I KNOW! I KNOW IT WAS ISLERO AND HIS REBELS! IT WAS THEY WHO KILLED MY HUSBAND!

¡EL SEÑOR NASH!

¡EL SEÑOR NASH! HE IS BACK!

EDWARD! EDWARD!

STAY BACK!

EDWARD!

LET GO OF ME! IT'S MY EDWARD! HE'S ALIVE! I'M IN NO DANGER!

NO! IT'S NO LONGER YOUR EDWARD...

LET ME GO, YOU BASTARD! EDWARD! COME!

COME TO ME, I BEG YOU!

YO SOY ISLERO, EL AMO DE LAS HORDAS NEGRAS*.

DEBO LIBERAR DEL ENEMIGO A LA TIERRA DE NUESTROS ANTEPASADOS... REGARE NUESTROS SURCOS CON LA SANGRE DE LOS OPRESORES**...

WILL YOU LET ME GO! DON'T YOU SEE HE'S GOING TO BURN? EDWARD! I LOVE YOU!

EDWARD! ED...

...Y ARROJARÉ SUS CUERPOS A LAS LLAMAS ETERNAS***.

WAARD!..

19

*I AM ISLERO, MASTER OF THE BLACK HORDES.
** I MUST FREE THE LAND OF OUR ANCESTORS FROM ITS ENEMY... WATER OUR FURROWS WITH THE BLOOD OF THE OPPRESSORS...
***...AND I WILL CAST THEIR BODIES INTO THE ETERNAL FLAMES.

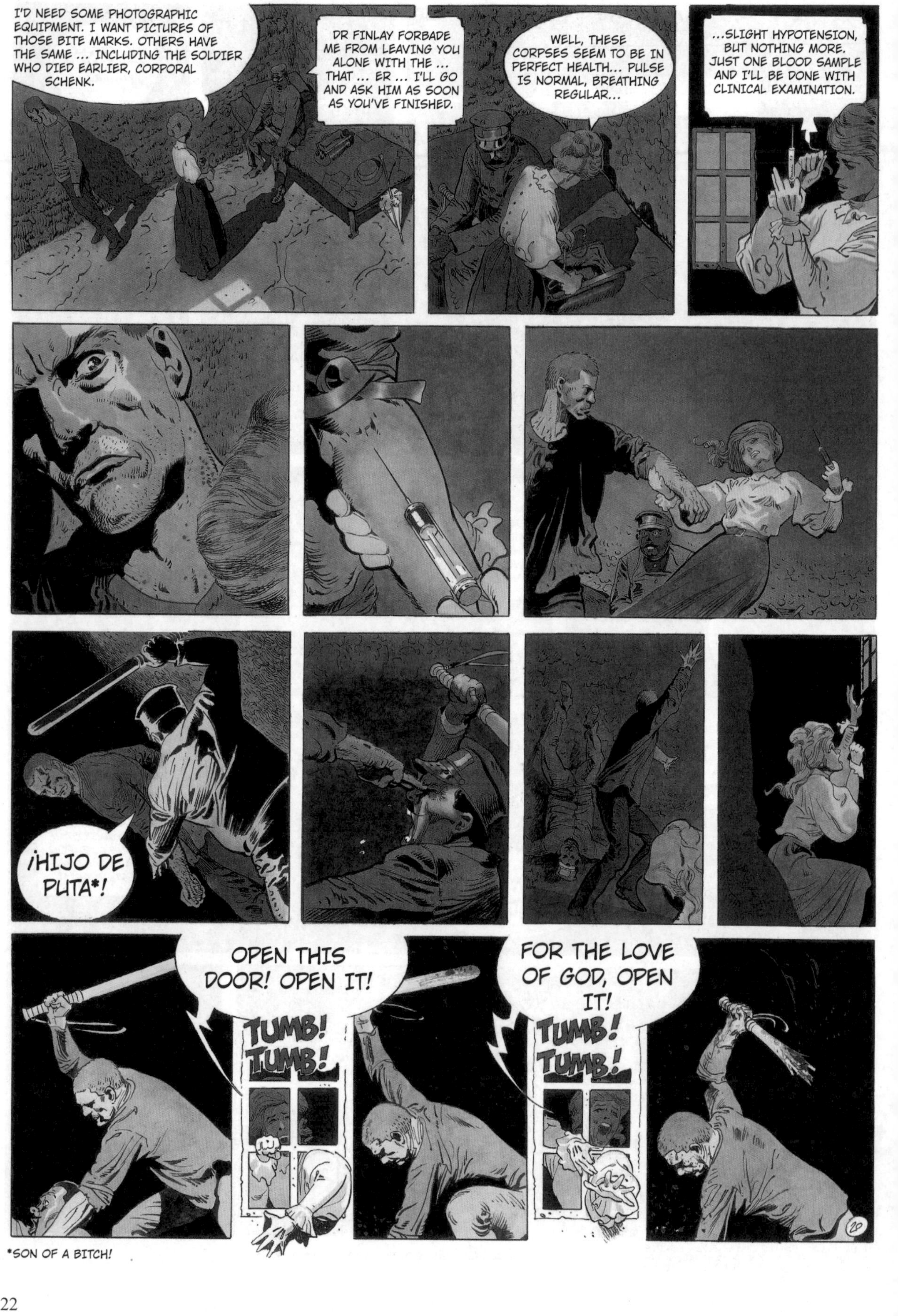
I'D NEED SOME PHOTOGRAPHIC EQUIPMENT. I WANT PICTURES OF THOSE BITE MARKS. OTHERS HAVE THE SAME ... INCLUDING THE SOLDIER WHO DIED EARLIER, CORPORAL SCHENK.
DR FINLAY FORBADE ME FROM LEAVING YOU ALONE WITH THE ... THAT ... ER ... I'LL GO AND ASK HIM AS SOON AS YOU'VE FINISHED.
WELL, THESE CORPSES SEEM TO BE IN PERFECT HEALTH... PULSE IS NORMAL, BREATHING REGULAR...
...SLIGHT HYPOTENSION, BUT NOTHING MORE. JUST ONE BLOOD SAMPLE AND I'LL BE DONE WITH CLINICAL EXAMINATION.
¡HIJO DE PUTA*!
OPEN THIS DOOR! OPEN IT!
TUMB! TUMB!
FOR THE LOVE OF GOD, OPEN IT!
TUMB! TUMB!
20

*SON OF A BITCH!

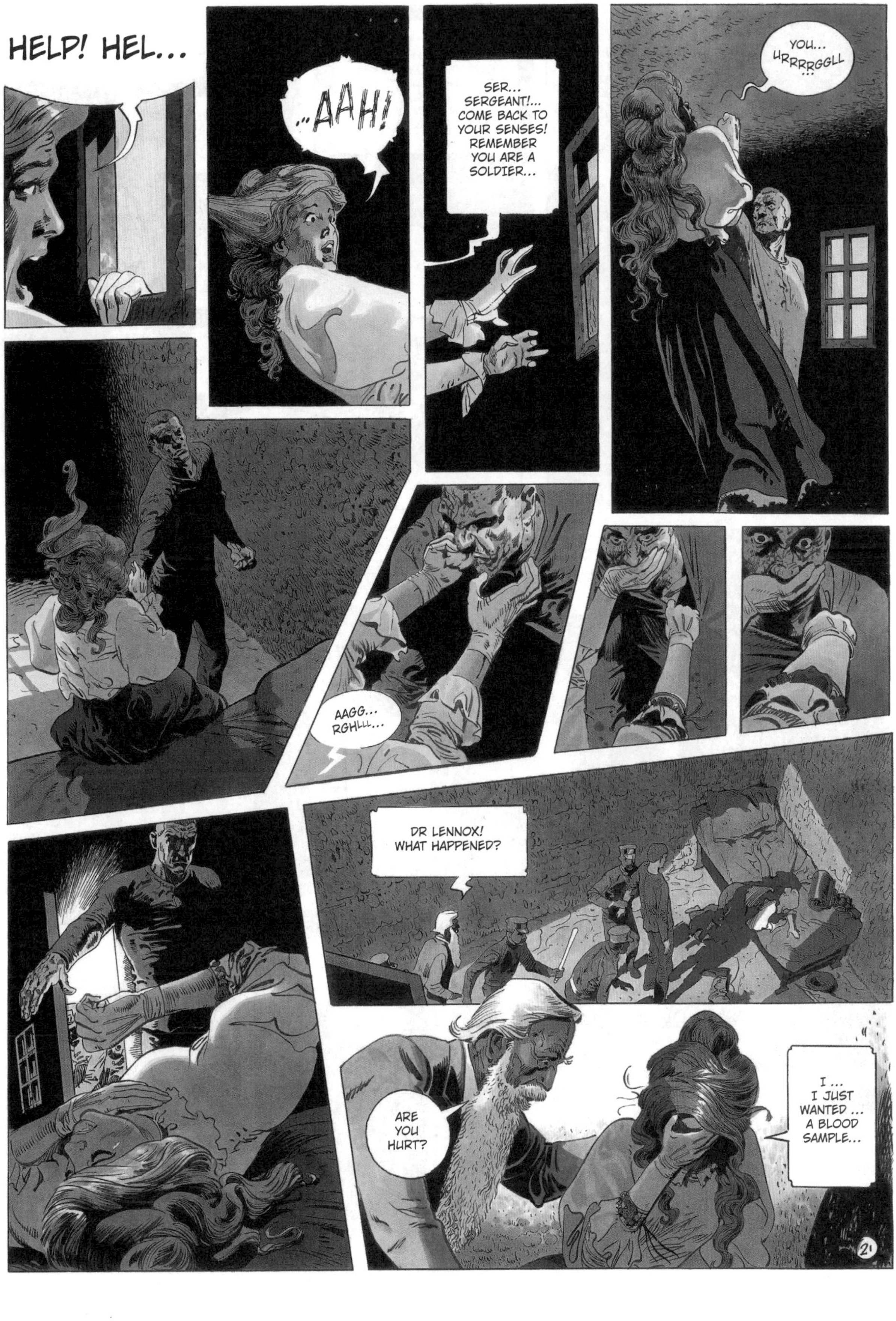
HELP! HEL...
..AAH!
SER... SERGEANT!... COME BACK TO YOUR SENSES! REMEMBER YOU ARE A SOLDIER...
YOU... URRRRGGLL...
AAGG... RGHLLL...
DR LENNOX! WHAT HAPPENED?
ARE YOU HURT?
I ... I JUST WANTED ... A BLOOD SAMPLE...

HMM... BART TRUMBLE... YOU WERE BORN IN DUBLIN ON 6 MARCH 1863 AND YOU LEFT IRELAND AFTER AN ATTACK ON BRITISH AUTHORITIES... HMM... RECEIVED AMERICAN CITIZENSHIP IN 1895...

MEMBER OF THE **IRB**... HMM... SUSPECTED OF PARTICIPATING IN THE PLOT THAT LED TO THE DEATH OF PRESIDENT MCKINLEY ON 6 SEPTEMBER 1901...

I'M IMPRESSED. AN INTERNATIONAL ANARCHIST PASSING THROUGH HAVANA... THAT DOESN'T HAPPEN EVERY DAY.

I DON'T UNDERSTAND A THING! I'M AN AMERICAN CITIZEN AND I'VE GOT R...

SHUT UP!

HERE IT'S ME, COLONEL WEYLER, WHO HAS ALL THE RIGHTS!

'I, BART TRUMBLE, HEREBY DECLARE THAT BARTOLOMEO MASÉ, CANDIDATE FOR THE CUBAN PRESIDENCY, HIRED ME TO ASSASSINATE HIS RIVAL CANDIDATE PALMA...'

'MASÉ ALSO ADMITTED TO AND BRAGGED ABOUT HIDING BEHIND THE PSEUDONYM ISLERO TO COMMIT THE RECENT ATTACKS AGAINST AMERICAN AUTHORITIES...'

DID YOU COME UP WITH THAT PILE OF SHITE?

NO, TRUMBLE ... YOU DID. YOU WROTE IT, AND NOW YOU'RE GOING TO SIGN IT.

I'LL DIE FIRST!

THAT'S PRECISELY THE ALTERNATIVE I'M OFFERING YOU.

!?! BUT LOOK AT THAT...

...SO YOU'RE AN INITIATE, THEN...

IT WAS ISLERO WHO GAVE IT TO YOU, WASN'T IT?

ISLEWHO?

I KNOW WHAT YOU'RE THINKING. YOU'VE BEEN THROUGH THIS KIND OF SESSION BEFORE AND YOU'VE NEVER CRACKED... BUT YOU'VE NEVER BEEN QUESTIONED BY ME.

WHO GAVE YOU THAT BRACELET?

A KID SOLD IT TO ME ON THE DOCKS FOR 25 CENTS. SAID IT WAS SOME SORT OF LUCKY CHARM.

㉒

YOU SEE, I DON'T BELIEVE THAT CUBA NEEDS INDEPENDENCE. WHAT WE NEED IS MONEY... AMERICAN DOLLARS!

THE PROBLEM IS THAT THE *YANQUIS* DON'T UNDERSTAND OUR TRADITIONS, OUR BELIEFS ... WHICH IS WHY THEY CALL UPON MEN LIKE ME.

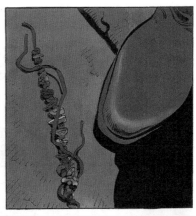

GNNNNNHHHHHHHHHH...

.." HHURRRAHRGNH..."

YOU MISERABLE RAT BASTARD! I FUCKED YOUR WHORE OF A MOTHER, YOU DIRTY...

YOU WILL TALK, TRUMBLE.

COUGH! COUGH! COUGH!

YOU WILL TELL ME WHO ISLERO IS. YOU WILL SIGN THE STATEMENT I READ YOU... ...AND AFTERWARDS YOU WILL BEG ME TO KILL YOU!

NO! NO! NO-O-O-O!

23

GET IT OFF ME! GET IT OFF...

...MEEEEEEEEE!

STOP RIGHT NOW!

LIEUTENANT FERRELL? HOW DARE YOU?

THE BAN ON SANTERIA APPLIES TO EVERYONE, COLONEL WEYLER. INCLUDING YOU.

WHAT?

HE'S WITH US, COLONEL.

WELL, NOW THE OTHERS WILL TRUST HIM.

PUT HIM BACK IN A CELL WITH CIANEGA AND THE OTHER REBELS.

NO! GET IT OFF!

BREATHE EASY...

...IT'S OVER – IT WAS JUST A NIGHTMARE...

A NIGHTMARE?! BUT I SAW IT, THAT...

COLONEL WEYLER HAS A GIFT FOR MAKING PEOPLE SUFFER. HE TORTURES YOUR BODY, BUT MORE IMPORTANTLY YOUR SOUL...

HERE, DRINK THIS. IT'LL HELP.

BLEUGH! WHAT IS THIS STUFF?

YOU DON'T WANT TO KNOW. BUT IT'LL CHASE AWAY THE BAD DREAMS...

HE SAYS YOU ARE VERY BRAVE. YOU'RE THE GRINGO WHO CAME TO HELP US, AREN'T YOU? THE COMBINE-HARVESTER MAN...

ES UN HOMBRE MUY BRAVO.

YEP. BUT AT THIS POINT, THERE'S NO WAY WE CAN KEEP PLAYING DEMOCRATS. I'M NOT GOING TO STAY HERE AND WAIT FOR THAT SADIST TO START MESSING WITH MY HEAD AGAIN... I'M GOING TO GET OUT OF HERE. NO, ACTUALLY... I'M GOING TO GET US ALL OUT OF HERE! THAT'S A BART TRUMBLE PROMISE.

THE TRICK WITH GUMBO IS TO LET IT SIMMER! AT LEAST THREE HOURS! THAT'S THE SECRET... SAY, YOU DON'T HAVE ANYTHING AGAINST SPICY FOOD, I HOPE?

HOW'S BART?

PEACHY... HE'S IN JAIL WITH THE OTHER GREASERS, AS PLANNED. I'M EXPECTING MY CONTACT AT THE PRISON ANY MINUTE NOW.

MHH...

COME ON, MAKE YOURSELF COMFORTABLE! THEY'RE NOT GOING TO DIE A SECOND TIME, THOSE ZOMBIES OF YOURS! OH, BY THE WAY, COURIER SAYS HELLO.

COURIER'S ARRIVED?

HE LEFT THIS FOR YOU, SO YOU'RE NOT LEFT ALL NAKED IN THIS LOUSY COUNTRY... HEY, WANNA HEAR A GOOD ONE ABOUT COURIER?

NO, BUT YOU'RE GOING TO TELL ME ANYWAY...

'WELL, SINCE COURIER IS OUR LIAISON WITH WASHINGTON, CLAYTON FOUND HIM A "COVER": REPORTER AT THE NEW YORK TIMES... BUT BECAUSE IT'S A SERIOUS NEWSPAPER, THEY'RE HAVING HIM WORK FOR REAL! AND THEY ASKED HIM FOR AN ARTICLE ON ... GUESS WHAT?'

'ON VICE IN CUBA!'... ISN'T LIFE GREAT?'

I DON'T SUPPOSE ANY OF YOU SPEAK ENGLISH...

AND ONE RUM WITH SUGAR-CANE SYRUP, ONE! IT'S MUCH BETTER THAN YOUR LAUDANUM GARBAGE FOR WHEN YOU'RE IN THE DOLDRUMS...

I AM **NOT** IN THE DOLDRUMS, BISHOP.

NO, OF COURSE... BUT LET'S SAY I KNOW WHAT IT'S LIKE TO LOSE YOUR FAMILY... A TOAST?

TO THOSE WHO'VE LEFT US ... AND TO US, WHO STAY BEHIND IN THIS SHITTY LIFE!

TO US.

TING!

25

27

TAKE YOUR MONEY BACK; THERE'S NOTHING MORE I CAN DO TO HELP YOUR FRIEND.... COLONEL WEYLER HIMSELF CAME TO QUESTION HIM. HE'S THE HEAD OF THE GUARDIA CIVIL AND ... HE'S A SANTERO!...

I HAD TO TELL HIM THAT YOUR FRIEND WAS UNDER COVER.

YOU DID **WHAT?**

WEYLER WAS TORTURING HIM! YOU... YOU DON'T KNOW WHAT HE'S CAPABLE OF!

BIG MISTAKE, BUDDY! COMPARED WITH ME, YOUR FRIEND WEYLER IS NOTHING!

BUT I...

NOTHING, I TELL YOU! NOTHING!

BISHOP!

YOU THINK ALL YOU HAVE TO DO IS RETURN THE CASH? YOU THINK I'M JUST GONNA LET YOU GO, YOU MORON? EITHER YOU HELP ME SPRING BART OUT OF THAT HOLE OR I...

KATHRYN?...

...WHAT?! COME BACK! YOU HAVEN'T EVEN TRIED MY GUMBO! COME ON! IT'S...

...IT'S JUST **THE JOB**...

?!!! CORPORAL SCHENCK?

26

WHERE IS IT?...
WHERE IS CORPORAL
SCHENCK'S BODY?

IT'S HERE
WITH THE
OTHERS, BUT
WHY?...

HE JUST
WALKED
PAST ME
IN THE
STREET.

HE...

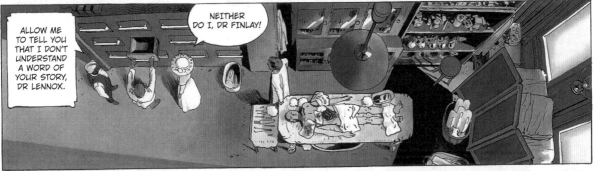

ALLOW ME
TO TELL YOU
THAT I DON'T
UNDERSTAND
A WORD OF
YOUR STORY,
DR LENNOX.

NEITHER
DO I, DR FINLAY!

?!... THIS
IS ISLERO'S
DOING!

TUK!

I'VE HAD MORE
THAN MY FILL OF THESE
SLEIGHTS OF HAND,
DOCTOR! **WHO** HAS
ACCESS TO THESE
BODIES?

WELL, ME,
FOR A START...
THE NURSES...

...AND COLONEL
WEYLER. HE PRAYS
BY EVERY SOLDIER
WHO DIES OF
YELLOW FEVER...
GENERAL WOOD'S
ORDERS.

29

YOU TIE IT ABOVE YOUR BED WITH COPPER WIRE AND ELEGBA WILL PROTECT YOU.

I ONLY TAKE AMERICAN DOLLARS.

PRACTISING SANTERIA IS ABSOLUTELY FORBIDDEN. POSSESSION OF OBJECTS LINKED TO THAT RELIGION — LET ALONE THEIR SALE — IS PUNISHABLE BY IMPRISONMENT...

...YOU SHOULD BE MORE DISCREET.

MORTON!

¡QUERIDO MÍO*! YOU SHOULD HAVE LET ME KNOW... I'D HAVE WELCOMED YOU BETTER.

AREN'T YOU WORRIED GENERAL WOOD WILL HAVE YOU ARRESTED?

THE YANQUI SOLDIERS ARE THE FIRST TO BELIEVE IN ISLERO. WOOD SHOULD TRY TO ENFORCE HIS DECREE... HE'LL HAVE TO LOCK UP THE WHOLE GUARDIA ALONG WITH HALF HIS ARMY!

HERE, FABIO. BRING US BACK A BOTTLE OF RUM. AND THE BEST.

WHAT BRINGS YOU HERE, MI CORAZÓN***? STILL LOOKING FOR CURES FOR YOUR DAUGHTER?

DO YOU KNOW THIS?

A SCAM. VERY EFFECTIVE TO SCARE THE WHITE FOLK. NOTHING MORE.

AND THIS SIGN? WHICH ORISHA*** DOES IT INVOKE?

I ... I DON'T KNOW.

*MY DARLING!
**SWEETHEART
***A SPIRIT OR DIVINITY IN THE YORUBA RELIGION — WHICH GAVE BIRTH TO MULTIPLE OTHER RELIGIONS SUCH AS SANTERIA.

YOU ... DON'T KNOW?

YOU KNOW EVERY ORISHA, MARIA. THIS ONE SCARES YOU... IT'S ISLERO'S, ISN'T IT?

SORRY, *MI CORAZÓN*... I'VE HEARD OF ISLERO, LIKE EVERYONE ELSE IN CUBA. BUT THAT'S ALL.

I'M JUST A BUSINESSWOMAN, MORTON. WE'RE NOT GOING TO FIGHT OVER THIS, ARE WE? AFTER ALL THE GOOD TIMES WE'VE HAD TOGETHER...

HEY, BOY! COME HERE!

MARIA DESERVES BETTER THAN YOUR ROTGUT.

TAKE THIS ONE INSTEAD — YOU'LL MAKE ME HAPPY.

AND NOT A WORD, UNDERSTOOD?

ATTACKS THE NERVOUS SYSTEM... TEMPORARY PARALYSIS... SUBJECT FALLS INTO A STATE OF APPARENT DEATH...

...I KNEW IT!

29

NO IMPORTA CUÁNTOS SEAN NUESTROS ENEMIGOS*...

NO IMPORTA NI SU FUERZA NI SU CIENCIA**...

...PORQUE YO OS LIBERO DE LAS TINIEBLAS, HIJOS MIOS... MIS HUESTES NEGRAS***.

SED LIBRES PARA DESENCADENAR TODA LA POTENCIA DE OGUN, PARA TRANSFORMER A NUESTROS ENEMIGOS EN SIMPLES TITERES****...

SUS SOLDADOS SERÀN NUESTRA ARMADA... SU FUERZA SERA NUESTRO PODER*****...

...Y SU CIENCIA, NUESTRA CIENCIA******.

㉚

*IT DOESN'T MATTER HOW MANY OUR ENEMIES ARE...
**NEITHER HIS STRENGTH NOR HIS SCIENCE MATTERS...
***...FOR I RELEASE YOU FROM THE DARKNESS, MY CHILDREN... MY BLACK HOST.
****BE FREE TO UNLEASH THE FULL POWER OF OGUN, TO TURN OUR ENEMIES INTO SIMPLE PUPPETS...
*****HIS SOLDIERS WILL BE OUR ARMY... HIS STRENGTH WILL BE OUR POWER...
******...AND HIS SCIENCE, OUR SCIENCE.

YOU'RE WRONG TO PROTECT ISLERO. FEAR IS ALWAYS A BAD COUNSELLOR.

DON'T YOU EVER GIVE UP?

AGAINST SUCH PEOPLE? NEVER. IT'S UP TO YOU WHETHER YOU WANT TO HELP ME OR NOT, BUT EITHER WAY I'LL FIND HIM IN THE END.

YOU'RE AS MAD AS THE ONE YOU SEEK. AS MAD AS ISLERO.

YOU WANT TO KNOW WHICH ORISHA HE INVOKED? IT'S THE ELDEST SON OF OBATALA, FATHER OF ALL GODS AND CREATOR OF OUR WORLD. IT'S THE ONE THAT EVEN THE GODS BANISHED...

...OGUN, MASTER OF THE BLACK SWARMS. HIS VERY NAME IS ALREADY BLASPHEMY.

I'M SUCH AN IDIOT...

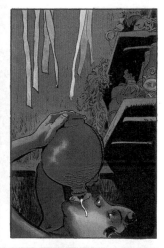

㉛

33

TRUMBLE! GET UP!

¡DÉJENNOS SOLOS*!

HERE. THIS IS ALL I CAN DO.

GO EASY... YOU'RE SUPPOSED TO KNOCK ME OUT, NOT CRIPPLE ME.

YOUR FRIEND BISHOP ALREADY SCALDED ME; I DON'T WANT TO...

AND THESE? D'YOU THINK THEY'RE GONNA MAGICALLY DISAPPEAR? I'LL KEEP THESE DAMN MARKS MY WHOLE LIFE!

'ERCY!... IT WA'N'T 'Y FAULT!

TAKE OFF YOUR UNIFORM; I DON'T WANT ANY BLOOD ON IT!

32

*LEAVE US!

THREE CENTS A POUND, SEÑOR.

I'LL TAKE THE WHOLE LOT, PLUS THE CART, THE DONKEY...

...AND YOUR THREADS.

VENGO A BUSCAR A UN PRISIONERO. ORDEN DEL CORONEL WEYLER*.

UNDO YOUR BELT, AMIGO.

YOU TWO, GET IN THERE AND PUT YOUR FACES TO THE WALL.

SO? ARE YOU COMING WITH ME OR STAYING HERE TO ROT?

¡OYE TÚ! ES PROHIBIDO ESTAR ALLÍ! SACA ESTA CARRETA, CABRÓN!**

GIDDY-UP, BIG EARS!

(33)

*I'M HERE TO GET A PRISONER. ORDER FROM COLONEL WEYLER.
**HEY, YOU! IT'S FORBIDDEN TO BE HERE! MOVE THAT CART, YOU FOOL!

TOO MANY BANANAS WILL KILL YOU!

NOBODY MOVE! REACH FOR THE SKY!

YOU FUCKING TRAITORS — IT'S YOUR TURN NOW...

NONE OF THAT, CIANEGA!

NO POINT IN WASTING AMMUNITION. WE'LL NEED IT TO GET OUT OF THIS HOLE.

TAKE THESE MEN INTO THE BARRACKS NEXT DOOR, AND TIE A SHEET TO THE BARS OF THE WINDOW.

HOW ARE WE GETTING OUT?

YOU'LL SEE.

WHERE'S COLONEL WEYLER?

HE... HE'S WITH GENERAL WOOD AT THE PRESIDENTIAL PALACE.

I'M GOING TO GIVE YOU A MESSAGE FOR YOUR COLONEL, BOYO. WHEN HE COMES BACK, TELL HIM THAT BART TRUMBLE HASN'T FORGOTTEN ABOUT HIM. YOU BE SURE TO TELL THAT SCUMBAG I'LL BE COMING BACK FOR HIM.

WHO-O-O-O-O-A!

END OF THE LINE!

34

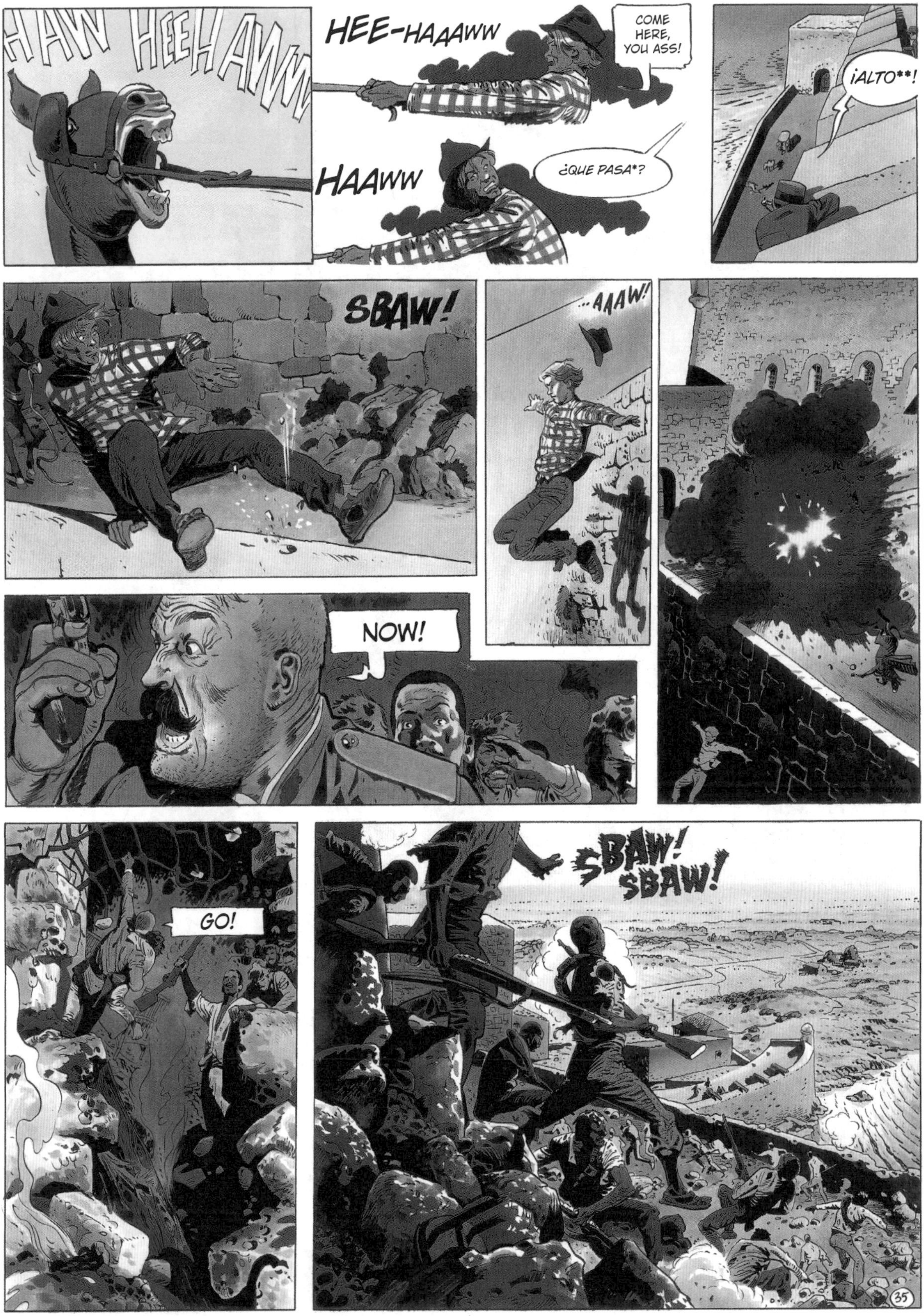
HAW HEEHAWW
HEE-HAAAWW
COME HERE, YOU ASS!
HAAWW
¿QUE PASA*?
¡ALTO**!
SBAW!
...AAAW!
NOW!
GO!
SBAW! SBAW!
35

*WHAT'S GOING ON?
**STOP!

SBAAAM!
...AAAM!

HOLD TIGHT, KID!

WE'RE GONNA NEED A SAFE HIDING SPOT.

TRUST ME, GRINGO! WHERE WE'RE GOING, NOBODY WILL COME TO FIND US!

STEP TWO ... COMPLETED.

I'VE BEEN TRYING TO REACH YOU FOR HOURS! I WAS TOLD YOU WERE AT THE GUARDIA'S ARCHIVES.

I WAS. AND I DIDN'T WASTE MY TIME. DO YOU KNOW WHY THE AMERICANS FOUND NOTHING ON ISLERO?

BECAUSE OF ARROGANCE AND STUPIDITY! THOSE IDIOTS COULDN'T BE BOTHERED TO LOOK THROUGH THE SPANISH ARCHIVES!...

I ... I MUST TALK TO YOU, CHAPEL. I FOUND...

LISTEN FOR A MINUTE! ISLERO IS A *CIMARRÓN*, A RUNAWAY SLAVE. NOBODY KNOWS HIS REAL NAME ... BUT ACCORDING TO WHAT I COULD FIND, HE'S PROBABLY A *MESTIZO**.

HE WAS ONE OF THE VERY FIRST SUPPORTERS OF INDEPENDENCE, AND LATER HELPED THE RANGERS FREE CUBA. BUT AFTER 1898 HE ISN'T HEARD OF AGAIN ... UNTIL THESE PAST FEW MONTHS.

CHAPEL, I KNOW HIS SECRET...

...I KNOW HOW HE MAKES HIS SO-CALLED REVENANTS...

...EVERY VICTIM OF THE YELLOW FEVER IS CARRYING A PARASITE THAT IS ONLY FOUND ON *CULEX PIPIENS* – MOSQUITOES.

MOSQUITOES? BUT I'VE BEEN BITTEN MANY TIMES...

NOT JUST ANY MOSQUITO. ONLY *AEDES* ALSO CARRIES TETRODOTOXIN, A POISON THAT WAS FOUND IN THE BLOOD OF EACH OF THE REVENANTS.

YELLOW FEVER WEAKENS THE IMMUNE SYSTEM TO THE POINT WHERE TETRODOTOXIN CAN INDUCE A DEEP LETHARGY. DEEP BUT REVERSIBLE...

THEIR NERVOUS SYSTEM IS PARALYSED, THEIR HEART STOPS BEATING ... BUT THEY'RE **ALIVE!** AND WHEN THEY REGAIN CONSCIOUSNESS, THEY ... THEY WAKE UP AT THE BOTTOM OF A GRAVE!

36

*MIXED RACE

THAT'S NOT ENOUGH. ISLERO IS MORE THAN JUST A MAN GOOD WITH POISONS. ANYONE WHO INVOKES OGUN IS NO ORDINARY SANTERO.

WHAT ABOUT COLONEL WEYLER?

WEYLER?

ACC ... ACCORDING TO LIEUTENANT FERRELL, HE'S ... HE'S A SANTERO. AND HE HAD ACCESS TO THE BODIES....

INCLUDING NASH'S...

WEYLER WOULD MAKE AN IDEAL S ... SUSPECT, BUT HE ... HE WORKS F ... FOR THE AMERICANS!

PRECISELY. WITHOUT THE THREAT OF ISLERO, THEY'D HAVE NO NEED OF HIM.

WELL DONE, KATHRYN! YOU'VE...

KATHRYN!

YOU'VE BEEN BITTEN, HAVEN'T YOU?

KATHRYN, ANSWER ME!

KATHRYN!

WHERE ARE WE GOING LIKE THIS?

YOU'RE GOING TO MEET EL JEFE!

ISLERO?

BETTER THAN THAT! ONE OF THE CHILDREN OF THE GREAT MACEO*!

IN THIS GODFORSAKEN HOLE?

BEST HIDING PLACE THERE IS.

③⑦

*HERO OF THE CUBAN INDEPENDENCE WAR (1895-98).

WHAT IS IT?... A MISSION?

SI, SEÑOR TRUMBLE ... AND ALSO A LEPER COLONY.

DON'T WORRY. DRY LEPROSY ISN'T CONTAGIOUS.

THERE ISN'T MUCH THAT CAN BE DONE FOR THE SICK. THE SPANISH GAVE US LITTLE HELP...

...THE AMERICANS ARE LETTING US DIE ALTOGETHER.

EL JEFE, I TAKE IT?

HIM? NO, NOT STRONG ENOUGH! EL JEFE...

...THAT'S HER.

38

40

I OWE YOU AN APOLOGY. I MISJUDGED YOU.

YOU'VE BECOME QUITE POPULAR – DESERVEDLY SO.

OH... 'TWAS NOTHING.

¡SI HUBIERA VISTO COMO DEJÓ LA PRISIÓN, SEÑORA**!

IT'S HIM!

¡EL GRINGO MAGNIFICO*!

YOU'VE GOT QUITE A COLLECTION OF LEAD PUSHERS FOR A BUNCH OF PACIFISTS!

BARTOLOMEO IS THE PACIFIST. HE'S THE ONE WHO'S OBSESSED WITH HIS ELECTIONS. AS IF THE YANQUIS WERE GOING TO GIVE HIM A CHANCE!

WHAT ABOUT YOU?

MY FATHER DIED FIGHTING FOR THE FREEDOM OF HIS PEOPLE. IF I MUST FOLLOW THE SAME PATH, I SHALL DO SO WITH PRIDE.

YOUR FATHER? THAT WAS MACEO THE LIBERATOR?! HE MUST HAVE FOUGHT ALONGSIDE ISLERO...

IT WAS ISLERO WHO GAVE MY FATHER THIS FLAG. HE HAD IT WITH HIM WHEN HE WAS MURDERED. HIS BLOOD IS STILL ON IT.

SOME DAY WE'LL FLY IT OVER THE PRESIDENTIAL PALACE ABOVE HAVANA. AND ON THAT DAY, BART TRUMBLE, I HOPE YOU'LL BE ONE OF US.

STEP THREE ... PIECE OF CAKE.

HE'S IN. IT SHOULDN'T BE MUCH LONGER UNTIL HE IDENTIFIES ISLERO. I HAVE TO WARN CHAPEL. YOU STAY RIGHT HERE, COURIER.

39

*THE MAGNIFICENT GRINGO!
**IF YOU COULD HAVE SEEN HIM AS WE LEFT THE PRISON, MADAM!

GOT THAT? DON'T TAKE YOUR EYES OFF MY BUDDY.

CROSS MY HEART – I WON'T MOVE FROM THIS SPOT!

T ... TIMMY... I'M HERE... WAIT FOR ME, LITTLE BROTHER ...

IT'S YELLOW FEVER. A PARTICULARLY VIRULENT BOUT.

WHICH MEANS?

HIGH FEVERS FIRST, ALONG WITH DELIRIUM AND HAEMORRHAGIC VOMITING... COMA WILL BE NEXT, AND THEN ... THE END.

FORGIVE ME, TIMMY ... FORGIVE ME...

SHE SPOTTED THESE MARKS ON OTHER PATIENTS. SHE HAS A THEORY ABOUT THEM...

...THE MOSQUITOES?... YES... IT'S ORIGINAL, BUT...

HERE. THESE ARE HER NOTES. SHE MENTIONS A POISON – TETRODOTOXIN, I THINK... MAYBE THIS WILL HELP YOU.

EVEN IF SHE'S CORRECT, THERE'S NO ANTIDOTE TO THAT POISON!

TAKE IT. READ IT.

THANK YOU. YOU HAVE MY WORD THAT I SHALL DO MY BEST ... BUT THERE'S LITTLE HOPE AT THIS STAGE.

LET ME PASS! I'M A GOVERNMENT AGENT!!!

THAT MAN IS WITH ME!

KATHRYN?

BUT WHAT IS G... WHAT HAPPENED TO HER?

CALM DOWN. COME WITH ME.

DR FINLAY THINKS IT'S YELLOW FEVER, BUT I DON'T THINK SO... KATHRYN WAS POISONED BY ISLERO!

40

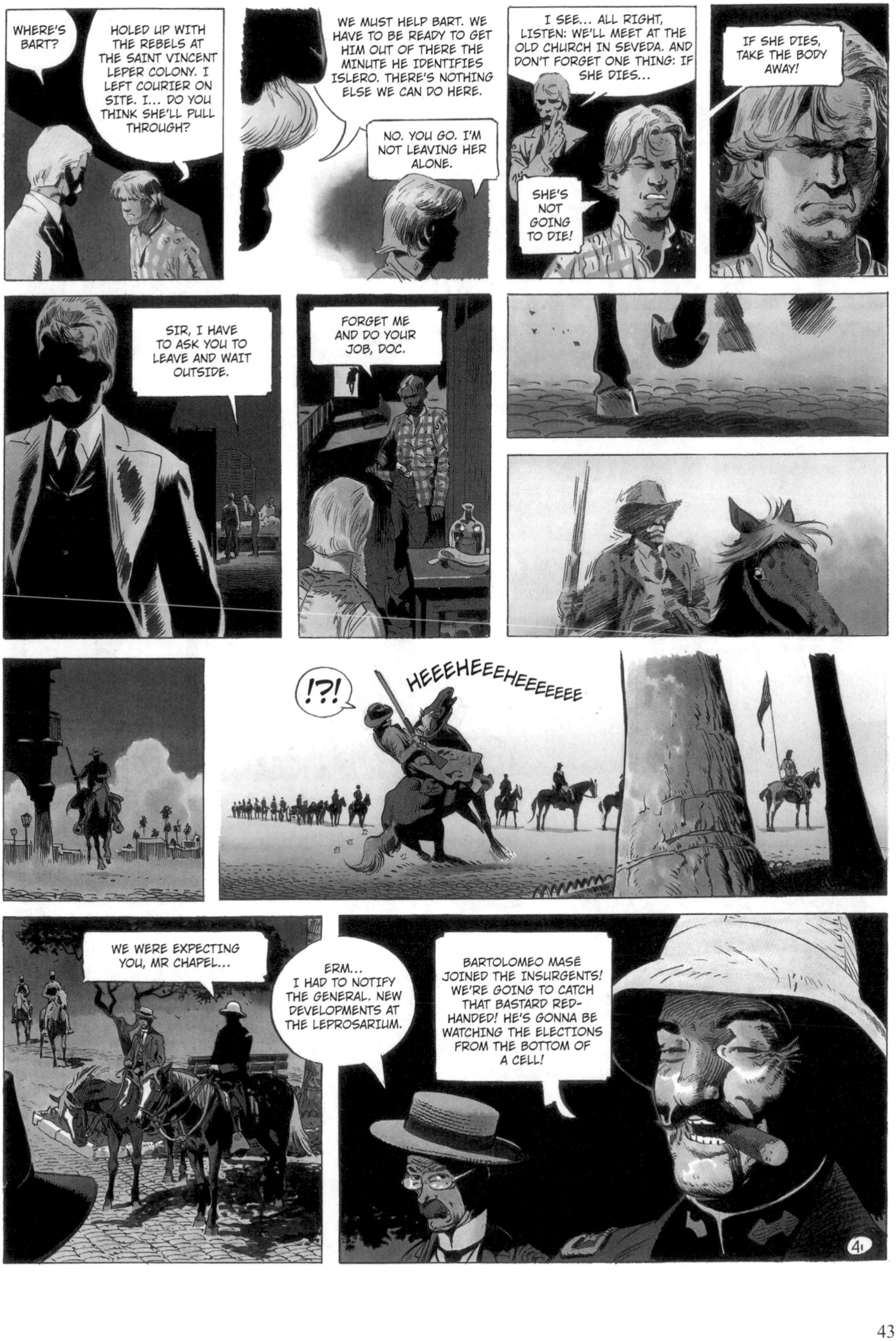
WHERE'S BART?
HOLED UP WITH THE REBELS AT THE SAINT VINCENT LEPER COLONY. I LEFT COURIER ON SITE. I... DO YOU THINK SHE'LL PULL THROUGH?
WE MUST HELP BART. WE HAVE TO BE READY TO GET HIM OUT OF THERE THE MINUTE HE IDENTIFIES ISLERO. THERE'S NOTHING ELSE WE CAN DO HERE.
NO. YOU GO. I'M NOT LEAVING HER ALONE.
I SEE... ALL RIGHT, LISTEN: WE'LL MEET AT THE OLD CHURCH IN SEVEDA. AND DON'T FORGET ONE THING: IF SHE DIES...
SHE'S NOT GOING TO DIE!
IF SHE DIES, TAKE THE BODY AWAY!
SIR, I HAVE TO ASK YOU TO LEAVE AND WAIT OUTSIDE.
FORGET ME AND DO YOUR JOB, DOC.
!?!
HEEEHEEEHEEEEEEE
WE WERE EXPECTING YOU, MR CHAPEL...
ERM... I HAD TO NOTIFY THE GENERAL. NEW DEVELOPMENTS AT THE LEPROSARIUM.
BARTOLOMEO MASE JOINED THE INSURGENTS! WE'RE GOING TO CATCH THAT BASTARD RED-HANDED! HE'S GONNA BE WATCHING THE ELECTIONS FROM THE BOTTOM OF A CELL!
41

ONE OF MY MEN INFILTRATED THE REBELS. IF YOU INTERVENE NOW, YOU'LL RUIN HIS CHANCES OF ARRESTING ISLERO.

HMM...

MR CLAYTON CLEARLY DEFINED THE MISSION'S PARAMETERS... NEUTRALISATION OF CANDIDATE MASÉ IS THE ABSOLUTE PRIORITY.

CLAYTON... THAT SWINE WILL NEVER CHANGE... AND HAVE YOU THOUGHT ABOUT WHAT COULD HAPPEN TO BART?

THE MAN NAMED BART TRUMBLE KILLED SEVERAL OF MY MEN DURING HIS ESCAPE. IF I WERE YOU I'D THINK CAREFULLY ABOUT COVERING FOR HIM... ALL YOU'LL GAIN FROM IT IS TO BE ARRESTED ALONG WITH HIM...

I BELIEVE THIS IS YOURS...

FROM ONE SANTERO TO ANOTHER...

¡ADELANTE CABALLEROS*!

ARE YOU PROUD OF YOURSELF? DO YOU KNOW WHAT YOUR 'EXPLOIT' HAS ACCOMPLISHED? IT'S PLAYED STRAIGHT INTO THE AMERICANS' HANDS!

*FORWARD, RIDERS!

44

WE WERE PRISONERS AND...

YOU'RE GIVING THEM THE PERFECT EXCUSE TO DECLARE MARTIAL LAW AND CANCEL THE ELECTIONS!

AND WHAT DIFFERENCE WILL THAT MAKE? THE *YANQUIS* WILL NEVER LET THE ELECTIONS TAKE PLACE NORMALLY! THEY KNOW TOO WELL WHAT THE RESULT WOULD BE.

OPEN YOUR EYES! THEY CONTROL THE POLLING STATIONS, THE ELECTORAL LISTS, THE COUNTING PROCESS... YOU'RE THE ONLY ONE WHO STILL BELIEVES IN IT!

MR MASÉ, THE PEOPLE ARE READY. ISLERO GAVE US FAITH. NOW IS THE TIME TO ACT!

NO, NO, NO! I REFUSE TO DRAG CUBA INTO A BLOODBATH! I'M TELLING YOU FOR THE LAST TIME: I WILL NOT TAKE POWER BY **FORCE!**

YOU WON'T EVEN HAVE TO GET YOUR HANDS DIRTY. JUST WAIT FOR US TO COME AND GET YOU. AND YOU CAN PLAY THE GREAT PACIFIST DEMOCRAT ... IF THAT'S WHAT FLOATS YOUR BOAT.

YOU...

...YOU COULDN'T HAVE DONE MORE GRIEVOUS HARM TO THE CUBAN CAUSE...

THEN WE'LL TAKE IT FOR YOU!

...IF YOU'D BEEN AN IMPERIALIST AGENT!

BARTOLOMEO!

DON'T YOU WORRY. HE'LL SEE THINGS DIFFERENTLY ONCE WE INSTALL HIM IN THE PRESIDENTIAL PALACE.

I HAVE TO MEET ISLERO... WE MUST COORDINATE OUR ACTIONS.

THAT'S IMPOSSIBLE. DON'T BE OFFENDED, SEÑOR TRUMBLE ... BUT ISLERO WILL NEVER AGREE TO SPEAK TO ANYONE ELSE BUT ME. I'M THE ONLY ONE WHO KNOWS HIS TRUE IDENTITY.

43

¡MIERDA*!

YOU KEEP VERY BAD COMPANY, BARTOLOMEO...

NO NEED TO USE FORCE, GENERAL. I CAN TALK THEM INTO SURRENDERING.

REBELS AND CRIMINALS... THEIR ESCAPE IS THE FINAL NAIL IN THEIR COFFIN!

AND IF ... IF I PULLED OUT OF THE ELECTION?

HMM... YES... EVEN CRIMINALS DESERVE A TRIAL.

LIEUTENANT FERRELL, BRING ME MR MASE'S STATEMENT SO THAT HE CAN SIGN IT.

A JOB SWIFTLY DONE... YOU CAN GO BACK TO WASHINGTON SOON, OLD BOY!

¡ELEGBA, USTED QUE SALE DEL MAR! ¡TODO SU CUERPO ES DE ORO PURO**!

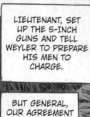

LIEUTENANT, SET UP THE 5-INCH GUNS AND TELL WEYLER TO PREPARE HIS MEN TO CHARGE.

BUT GENERAL, OUR AGREEMENT WITH MASE?...

MASE IS MORE USEFUL TO US ALIVE AND HUMILIATED THAN AS A DEAD MARTYR...

...AS FOR THE OTHER REBELS ... WE'RE GOING TO GIVE THEM A LESSON THE CUBANS WILL NEVER FORGET!

*SHIT!
**ELEGBA, YOU WHO COME FROM THE SEA! YOUR WHOLE BODY IS MADE OF PURE GOLD!

46

SUS PENDIENTES SON DE ORO PURO*.

YOU'RE SEEING THE VIRGIN MARY, BUT TO US SHE'S ELEGBA, ORISHA OF FERTILITY AND PROTECTOR OF CHILDREN.

SUS ANILLOS SON ORO PURO, PATRONA**.

ISELA IS ALLOWING HERSELF BE POSSESSED BY HER TO CURE OUR SICK.

TAMBIÉN LA CADENITA DE SU CUELLO***.

QUE ÉSTE ORO SEA COMO SU AMOR****...

QUE ESE AMOR SEA COMO SU ORO*****...

...Y QUE SERA ETERNO******.

THAT'S A PEACEFUL CEREMONY, WEYLER.

A HUNDRED YEARS AGO, A SIMILAR CEREMONY TOOK PLACE IN HAITI, IN BOIS CAÏMAN... IT BEGAN WITH PEACEFUL DANCING AND SINGING ... THEN A WITCH DOCTOR INVOKED OGUN.

AND THE TROOPS SENT BY NAPOLEON WERE UNABLE TO STOP THEM...

IN THE SPACE OF A FEW HOURS HE FIRED UP THE CROWD. HE TURNED FEARFUL SLAVES INTO RAVENING BEASTS BENT ONLY ON PILLAGING, KILLING AND RAPING THEIR FRENCH MASTERS.

...I KNOW THE STORY.

IT HAPPENED TO HAITI. IT WON'T HAPPEN TO CUBA.

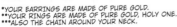

*YOUR EARRINGS ARE MADE OF PURE GOLD.
**YOUR RINGS ARE MADE OF PURE GOLD, HOLY ONE.
***ALSO THE CHAIN AROUND YOUR NECK.

****MAY THIS GOLD BE LIKE YOUR LOVE...
*****MAY THAT LOVE BE LIKE YOUR GOLD...
******...AND IT SHALL BE FOR EVER.

IT'S OVER.

NO...

NO! NO!

KATHRYN... YOU CAN'T LEAVE LIKE THIS! YOU'RE GONNA FIGHT! WE ... WE NEED YOU!

D'YOU HEAR ME? I'M NOT LETTING YOU GO LIKE THAT! IT'D BE TOO EASY! KATHRYN!

STOP IT, IT'S NO USE ANY MORE.

YOU STAY THE HELL AWAY!

GUAAAAAARDS! HELP!

I'LL BE BACK, KATHRYN! I SWEAR ON MY LIFE... I'LL BE BACK FOR YOU.

ARREST THIS MAN!

DON'T MOVE!

OK... OK...

46

!!?

B... BUT ... DON'T LET HIM ESCAPE!

HAAAALT!

PAW!

PAW!

DZZZZZZ

GENERAL, I'M ASKING YOU ONE LAST TIME TO GIVE ME A CHANCE TO WARN MY AGENT...

IMPOSSIBLE. I CANNOT RISK LOSING THE ELEMENT OF SURPRISE.

GUNNERS, ON MY COMM....

GENERAL!

YAAAAAH!

FIRE! SHOOT THAT TRAITOR!

BAAART!

BAAAAARRT

PAW! PAW!

47

49

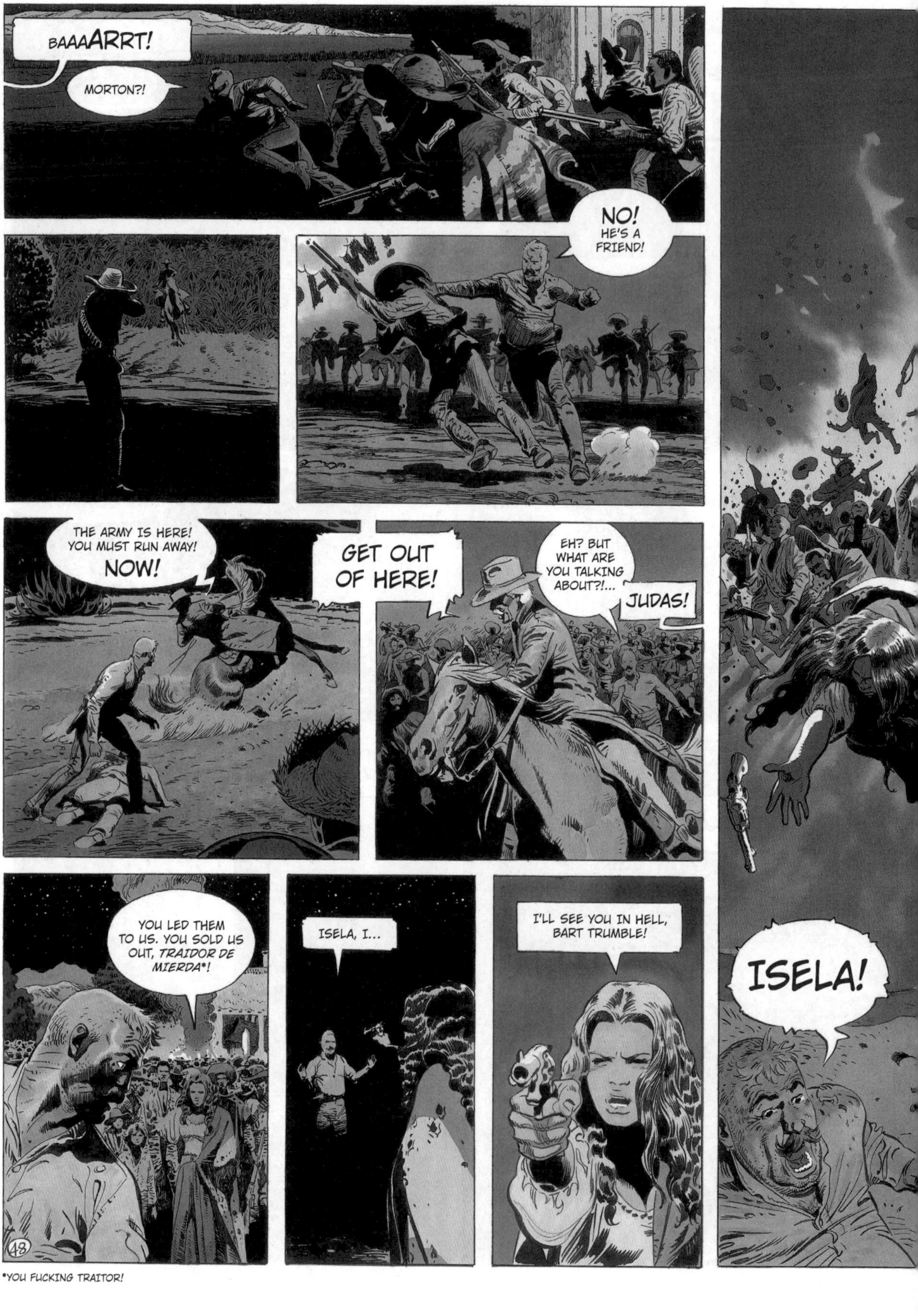
BAAAARRT!
MORTON?!
NO! HE'S A FRIEND!
THE ARMY IS HERE! YOU MUST RUN AWAY! NOW!
GET OUT OF HERE!
EH? BUT WHAT ARE YOU TALKING ABOUT?!...
JUDAS!
YOU LED THEM TO US. YOU SOLD US OUT, TRAIDOR DE MIERDA*!
ISELA, I...
I'LL SEE YOU IN HELL, BART TRUMBLE!
ISELA!
48

*YOU FUCKING TRAITOR!

OW!
ISELA! ANSWER ME!

LOOK! LOOK AT WHAT YOU'VE DONE!

BUT...! I DIDN'T... NO! ISELA! ISELA!

BART!
THIS REALLY ISN'T THE TIME TO HANG ABOUT!

CIANEGA!

¡VAMOS A MATAR, COMPAÑEROS*!

THEY'RE GONNA GET MASSACRED!

IT'LL BUY THE OTHERS A LITTLE TIME!

*LET'S GO AND KILL, COMPANIONS!

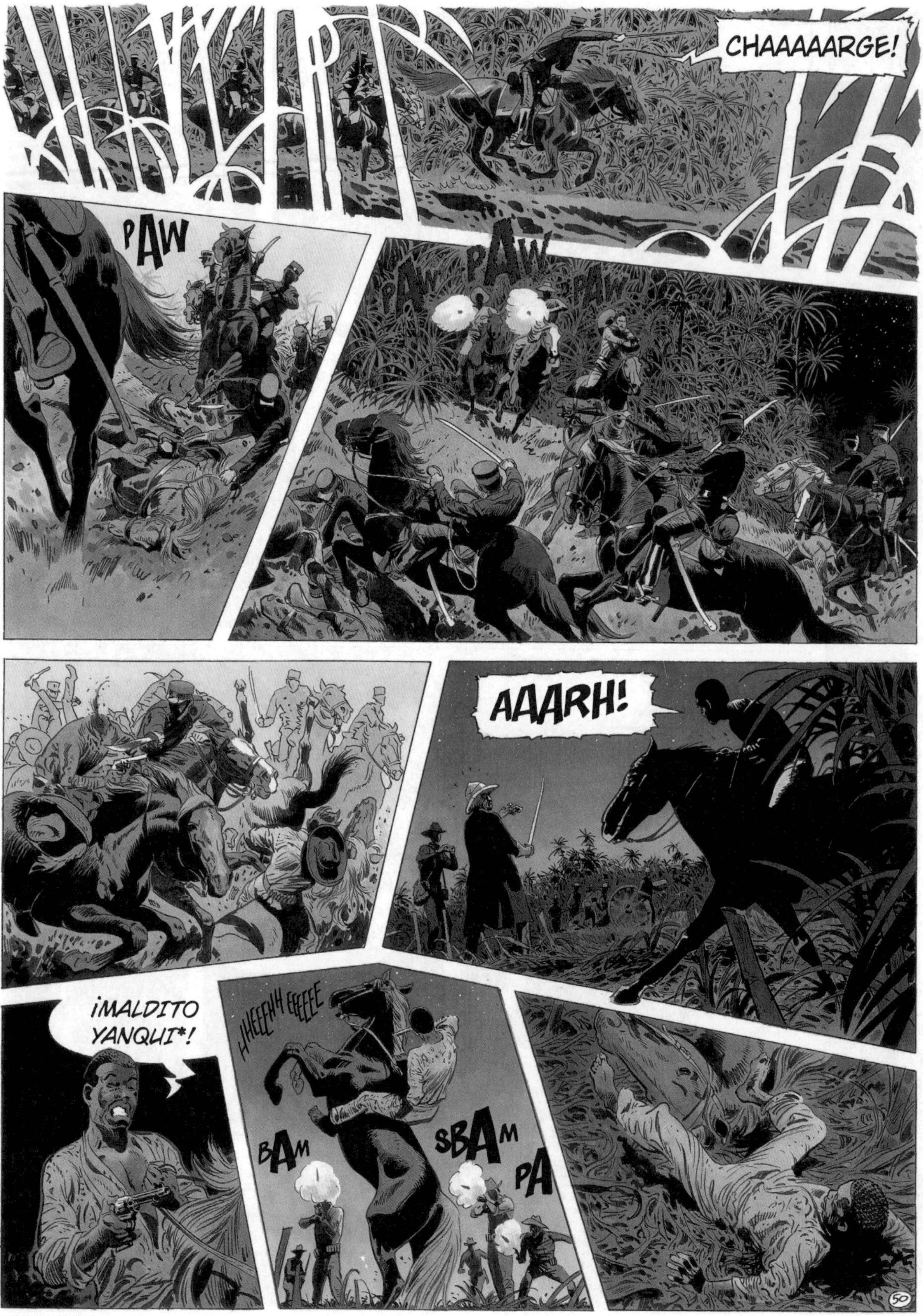
CHAAAAARGE!
PAW
PAW PAW PAW
AAARH!
¡MALDITO YANQUI*!
BAM
SBAM
PA
50

*DAMNED YANKEE!

DON'T MISTAKE....

...A SMALL LEPER COLONY...

...FOR THE ALAMO.

THEY RAN AWAY, COLONEL.

BURN THAT FIELD OF LOCUSTS!

SHIT! THEY'RE SETTING FIRE TO THE SUGAR CANE!

WEYLER IS GOOD AT WHAT HE DOES... HEY, LOOK THERE!

ISELA!

51

53

PAW!

ISELA! THIS WAY!

ISELA...

YOU'LL FIND HER LATER. THE GUARDIA ARE ALMOST UPON US!

BART ... PLEASE ...

GIDDY-UP!

52

KIDS... THEY KILLED KIDS...

I DID WHAT I COULD, BUT ... WE KNEW THE RISKS. I'M SORRY, BART.

SORRY?! ALL OF THIS IS BECAUSE OF YOU! YOU SENT ME TO SPY ON THEM! YOU GOT THEM SLAUGHTERED!...

FOR GOODNESS' SAKE, BART, I NEVER WANTED THIS! IT WAS CLAYTON! HE DOUBLE-CROSSED US!

YOU SHOULD HAVE THOUGHT OF THAT BEFORE! IT'S ALWAYS THE SAME ONES WHO BLEED! I'VE HAD ENOUGH!... IT'S YOUR TURN THIS T... OW!

BART ... DON'T FORCE ME TO...

I'M GONNA GUT YOU! HEY!

KATHRYN'S DEAD.

TINK

53

IT'S NOT FOR LACK OF WARNING YOU, 'DR' LENNOX.

SUCH A PITY YOU DIDN'T LISTEN...

THAT SAID, I'LL GRANT YOU YOUR RESEARCH WAS MOST INTERESTING. A LITTLE TOO INTERESTING, FOR MY LIKING.

YOU WERE CORRECT. THE ZOMBIES AREN'T TRULY DEAD. THEY SEE EVERYTHING, HEAR EVERYTHING, FEEL EVERYTHING. BUT WITHOUT MY ORDER...

...THEY CANNOT ACT.

DORISON + NURY + ROSSI

54

TO BE CONTINUED...